The Boss' Interview:

How to Separate the Job-Seeking "Pretenders" from the High-Quality "Contenders"

John L. Gray

ISBN-10: 1507744072
ISBN-13: 978-1507744079

DEDICATION

To the intentional, prepared, and professional executives and managers who make positive differences in the world and change people's lives for the better with their decisions

TABLE OF CONTENTS

DISCLAIMER

The employer should research the laws and court decisions and consult their legal counsel and human resources professionals about hiring and selection issues and laws that affect their jurisdiction to make certain that their actions are within the current law and best professional practices. Local laws and administrative rules vary between jurisdictions and though the author has made a good faith effort to present only the best information that is legal at the time of publishing, the author does not claim that all of the information contained in this publication is legal or appropriate for every state, city or political jurisdiction. All of this information is presented for illustrative uses only and may or may not be appropriate for your setting or jurisdiction.

PROLOGUE

I have had the privilege to hire police officers that are continuing to make a difference in the community and be "owners" of their agency. All of these hires were intentional and deliberate; the success of the hiring process was not luck. Since retiring from a full-time career in police management, I have specialized in helping agencies identify who their next generation of leaders are by developing effective, fair and defensible selection processes. This service has brought me face to face with some of the best leaders in public service.

My intention with this work is to share the collective wisdom and the successes and the lessons learned from experience. My mission is help leaders improve their organizations and provide the best service to their communities by selecting the right people.

Are these "trade secrets" and will they be used by candidates to "beat the system?" The answer is: doubtful. Though there are unsavory candidates who will work very hard at creating a persona to please the interviewer and will probably do anything to get hired, the act of the deception will reveal itself to the seasoned and prepared manager. Even if a candidate studies, memorizes and rehearses answers on the topics that this work contains, the incredible power of the dynamics of human communication, of uncontrollable non-verbal behavior, and the huge stream of data that the interviewer is receiving, will make any contrived performance detectable.

The hiring steps are a process with multiple eyes evaluating a candidate using different strategies to discover the candidate's multiple dimensions. Never rely upon one step or one set of eyes to make the determination if the information is contradictory or inconclusive. The steps of hiring for a public safety agency are often the most complex: Written Test for minimal skills, Physical Agility Test, Screening Interview for minimal communication skills and maturity, Psychological Testing for suitability, Background Investigation for integrity and performance, and Medical Examination. The selection process continues with the training and performance evaluations and finally the probation process. A candidate may fool the few, but will always stumble in the marathon of doing these steps.

PART 1: GETTING STARTED

Chapter 1

INTRODUCTION & METHODOLOGY

The two most important and most expensive decisions that you will make as the leader of your organization is who will join it and who will be promoted to higher levels of responsibility. This work is intended to assist the employer with making the best decision in determining who should join their organization. Though this book sometimes uses the job titles of "Chief," "Director," or "Chief Executive Officer," any job title that identifies the position that has the authority to make a hiring decision can be inserted. The information in this book was developed based upon my knowledge and experience gained from decades of involvement in the public sector but these are easily transferrable to the private sector. Therefore, do not be put off by the terminology used. Instead, look at the concepts and the ideas and then adjust them to your setting and your style.

This book is not intended to provide a strict formula or recipe that guarantees success in hiring the right person. What is offered is only another tool that is offered for your professional toolbox and your continued professional improvement.

The first two sections of this work is about creating an interview and conversation that is done by the top leadership to help identify the top candidate and weed out the ones that are not qualified, while imparting the values of the organization and setting the stage for commitment and loyalty to the leadership. This is called the "The Different Approach to the Boss' Interview."

The third section are ideas on how to do the traditional command or leadership interview that is done after all the selection steps are completed and the candidate is awaiting final approval. In this interview, the interviewer has all the documentation and information that was assembled by others.

Being a book, there are opportunities to add your own thoughts and notes. Have a pad ready to record your ideas and inspirations or make notes on these pages. As the layers of this topic are revealed and explored, you will be able to better create a product that will be successful for you. Here is your first opportunity:

Now it is your turn. List the things that you like about your current approach to interviewing candidates that you do not want to change or things that really work for you.

A Different Approach to the Boss' Interview

What is <u>different about the approach</u> to this topic from what you may be currently doing, and what you will take-away from this experience:

1. **The change of where this interview and conversation occurs in the selection process.** Traditionally, most interviews by the organization's leader are done at the very end of the hiring process. I am suggesting putting this interview and conversation toward the beginning for reasons that will be explained later.

2. **Deliberately using questions and discussing topics in a specific sequence** because these create and uses stress, in a good way, and then offers comfort to the candidate that can help the interviewer gain the most useful information and do so more quickly. This often results in the quicker identification of quality candidates and the elimination of marginal ones.

3. **Move the "interview" to a "conversation"** where the agency's core values and principles are introduced by the leader when the impact can be greatest.

When to do this Interview & Conversation

Rather than putting this interview and conversation at the end of the selection process, wise leaders with limited resources often put this as the next step in the hiring process, after the screening tests and oral board interviews but <u>before</u> the other testing elements like the polygraph examination, psychological assessments and the background investigation. Putting this interview before the in-depth probe into the candidate's background will save time and money because the candidates who are not qualified, who would be "weeded out" because of disqualifying behaviors anyway, are identified earlier and this allows the organization to focus quicker on the quality candidate.

The value of this interview cannot be overstated but it is also an opportunity that is most commonly missed. Many leaders of organizations do not prepare for this interview well, preferring to "fly by the seat of their pants" and make up questions and topics as the interview unfolds. This is particularly true when the leader hires only a few people a year.

In my experience of 12 years as a Police Chief, 50% of the candidates either voluntarily withdrew or were disqualified following my 90-minute interview. These candidates had often earned top scores on the written tests and the oral boards but would have been disqualified anyway for mandatory disqualifying behavior but only after spending thousands of dollars and weeks of time in the background investigation.

Doing this interview sooner and learning about the candidate's background problems or that the candidate's desires were not a fit for the agency, allowed me to move on to the other qualified candidates who were a better fit for the department. The number of top candidates or contenders is a small pool that changes quickly and these candidates often are being looked at by multiple agencies. Being able to move quickly on selecting the contenders was appreciated by the employees and the candidate.

Now it is your turn. List your ideas of when this interview could happen that is more productive but fits the processes that you have to live with.

Be Deliberate

Would you buy a house or enter into a long-term agreement without being thoroughly prepared? Hiring an employee is no different because this is the most expensive business decision the organization's leader will make. Therefore, this interview and conversation should reflect the best effort in this decision making process.

To that end, you can use a structured format to learn about the most salient parts about the candidate and to teach them about your organization. The format that is presented here is intended to make the candidate comfortable, set the expectation that they will be truthful, and then drill down on their <u>motivation, attitude, and background</u>.

These three traits, **motivation, attitude and their background,** will be the foundation for their success in your organization or will be the root of their future performance problems that <u>may</u> cost your organization tens of thousands of dollars in time and effort to move them out of the organization; an effort that may have been prevented by a better selection process.

The intended dynamic in this structured interview and conversation is for the candidate to willingly and quickly reveal information about their weaknesses relating to performing the job or are concerns to the employer. You should already know some of the candidate's strengths because these were identified by their written test scores, their experience and education as described on the application or resume, and their oral communication scores earned at the oral board interview. The dynamic during this interview and conversation is created by a certain sequence of questions, the sharing of the agency's principles and values, describing the boundaries of appropriate behavior, and then eliciting the candidate's agreement to all of these.

A Conversation

An interview is often a one-way revelation of information; the employer probes and the candidate responds with information. A conversation is a two-way process of mutual discovery between the participants that creates understanding for both parties. Trust is earned and built upon, more information is voluntarily revealed by the candidate in the pursuit of gaining and maintaining trust and gaining understanding. Candidates are hungry for information because they often know little or nothing about what happens behind the employer's door. They want to know about the expectations, how to succeed, why others have failed, and what the future may bring for them.

When you share the organization's values and principles with the candidate, their thirst for information will become more satisfied, they will start making judgments about their level of commitment to the organization and in return, you will learn more about them. Moving this event from an interview to a conversation is beneficial to both parties.

The Methodology

The methodology that is presented is borrowed, in part, from the science and art of conducting interrogations and from the research and practice of crisis or hostage negotiators who are seeking the safe resolution of a crisis. This methodology is not about manipulating or coercing the candidate; it is about removing obstacles, getting past practiced responses, the interviewer doing the unexpected, carefully observing the candidate on how they respond (in addition to the words they choose), and getting agreement and commitment to values and principles that channels their subsequent responses. A successful process is creating a climate where they are comfortable in revealing more about themselves rather saying what they think the employer wants to hear.

Chapter 2

THE PHYSICAL SETTING

The foundation for a successful interview and conversation begins with the proper interview room setting. The room should be carefully selected because the candidate will learn about your organization and, therefore, make a powerful initial judgment about you and your team from this setting. You want this judgment to be in your favor. Also, the power of the methodology that is described later can be diminished or enhanced by the room setting.

The interview and conversation should be done in a place that is free of interruptions and distractions and yet has the symbols of the organization and its values for the candidate to see. If the office of the organization's leader is used, it should be clean and uncluttered. The phone should be switched to silent and calls routed to voice mail. Disable the computer's audible alert that email has arrived. Close or draw down the window shades for two reasons: to achieve privacy but also to eliminate the opportunity for the candidate to gaze out the window while thinking under stress. Projecting attention and focus through a window and into a greater space is a method to reduce stress and anxiety.

The methodology of this interview is to use doses of intentional stress to reveal the candidate's true self. Eliminating the possibility of reducing that stress helps this dynamic to succeed.

Do not use a common area like a lunchroom or a coffee bar business because this is serious business and the setting should reflect it. When planning for this setting, mentally use the guiding principle that, "What is said here, stays here" because this will help the candidate feel more comfortable in revealing their mistakes and character flaws. Do not use a large conference room because you may lose the power of proximity in creating the intimate conversation.

Great conversations happen when the parties are within three to five feet of each other and in an intimate setting. A large conference room is generally not conducive to an intimate conversation. On the other hand, do not use a room designed for suspect interrogations because the candidate is not a suspect; they may be your next star team member.

The interview setting should have an even and comfortable lighting. The room temperature should be a comfortable 68 to 70 degrees. The room should be free of preventable noise distractions like machinery, radio traffic, music and intercoms because every distraction is an opportunity to break the momentum and the focus of the moment. Comfortable chairs should face each other and placed behind a table. Facing the candidate in a frontal approach focuses the power of eye contact and allows you a better view of their non-verbal language that is at least 60% of the candidate's message. The desk or table should be cleared off except for the paper work that is relevant to this event. The cleanliness and orderliness of the office should be the standard that the leader wants to see throughout the organization. During the interview and conversation, keep the door closed and do not accept interruptions from anyone.

Now it is your turn. Think about your interview room setting. Then, make some notes on what you can do to improve it.

Chapter 3

THE PARTICIPANTS IN THE CONVERSATION

To be most effective, you should wear the organization's uniform or be the best reflection of the organization's dress code or expectations and if any other staff is present, they should be dressed to the same expectation. In fact, your clothing, appearance and hygiene should be the best reflection of your organization's standards and the profession. Your presence is sending a strong message; one that will be heard louder and be more remembered than any words you say and these will be the loudest communication about your values and the organization's values.

Any member of the organization's management team that has the delegated authority to make decisions of this magnitude can effectively do this interview and conversation. In fact, in larger organizations, it may not be practical for the organization's leader to do this interview and conversation. But for the majority of organizations that have, say, less than 40 employees, the leader should be able to do this important interview and conversation.

Why should the boss do this interview? In the smaller organization, the boss will have more impact on the candidate than any other employee at this phase of the selection process. Candidates do not expect to talk with the Chief Executive early in the selection process and the feedback received is the appreciation of care and commitment that the organization has in the candidate.

What happens when the leader does this interview is the creation of a dynamic that increases the candidate's desire to be completely truthful and forthcoming because the leader is showing the organization's full force and authority while creating an environment for an effective conversation about the agency's values and mission. In this setting, the "pretender" candidate will often fail and the "contender" candidate will generally shine.

How many interviewers should participate in this experience and still make it successful for both the candidate and the employer? No more than two. Three representatives of the employer will create a tribunal effect and this feels more like an oral board rather than a conversation. The candidate will more likely stay in "performing" mode as they strive to please all the interviewers and the candidate will adjust their responses to the perceived needs of the different questioners. You want to create a climate for an intimate conversation with the candidate. This dynamic will naturally begin to take hold after about 30 minutes of talking, listening and sharing with one interviewer. More participants will dilute this dynamic or prevent it. Simply, you do not want too many cooks in the kitchen.

The role of the other participant should be carefully planned and the expectations discussed before the interview. For intimacy and trust to develop, there should be one principal interviewer and a passive one. The principal interviewer should be the person of the highest position within the organization because of the reasons mentioned before: they carry the weight of authority that has the most powerful influence with the candidate.

The most effective role of the passive participant is to observe and report later. They will see and hear things that the principle interviewer may miss and they will be the important sounding board to help put the proper weight upon the important things. In this respect, two heads are better than one.

The passive participant should not interrupt the flow of the conversation. Though you may tempted to split up and share the questions, this can create the untended consequence of keeping the candidate off-balance which does not create trust nor confidence and may keep the candidate in a performing role and be a barrier to seeing the genuine candidate.

Now it is your turn. Add your notes and ideas on who you want to team with for these interviews and what instructions or guidance you would give them in order to better support you:

PART II: ELEMENTS TO CREATE YOUR BOSS' INTERVIEW

Chapter 4

OPENING COMMENTS TO SET THE RIGHT TONE

The candidate typically comes to the interview with their agenda of showing their strengths and the intention of minimizing or avoiding their weaknesses and mistakes. Most will have read some material on how to interview well, rehearsed their desired first impressions, are often prepared for the standard interview questions that they got from the Internet and have decided how they are going to handle their difficult topics. Containing these prepared answers and behavior for the interview will have added to their nervousness and some candidates seem ready to explode with the information that they want you to hear.

The beginning of this interview and conversation is intended to help the candidate feel comfortable and by offering them the opportunity to "release" their prepared answers because this provides the opportunity for the unprepared answers that will come later and these will reveal the candidate's true motivation for the job and glimmers of their character.

For the first few minutes of this meeting, the candidate will have a decreased ability to hear your questions and to remember details because of their initial stress of being interviewed, and being in a unfamiliar setting with new and important people who they desire to impress. Therefore, try to not rush to a judgment when the candidate needs a question repeated or acts like they are not fully listening and understanding at the beginning of the interview. When you allow them some time to take-in the setting and become more comfortable with the interviewers, their "ear shutters" will gradually open.

Candidates will often enter the interview setting at that the "top of their game" or, in other words, they have mentally prepared for this moment and therefore they are "performing" to the best of their ability.

This is not the time to accept your first impression and jump to a conclusion because what you are seeing is typically not who they really are but rather only a small slice of the total package. Rather, use these first couple of minutes to introduce, in a high-elevation perspective, how this conversation is going to happen.

For example, you could say,

"Thank you for coming to see me today. We have one vacancy on our team and this happened because we had a veteran, Ed, who retired after 27 years of service. You tested well and I am interviewing the top number of candidates to determine who is the right fit for us and forward them on to the remainder of the selection process. My intention today is to ask you some questions so I can learn about you, but also to share with you the things that I think you should know

about us. This is more than an interview; it is a conversation between you and I because you should be evaluating us to determine if we are the best fit for you. Does that make sense?"

This short narrative sets the tone of the conversation and gives the candidate a sense of what to expect. Describing your intentions also sets the boundaries, takes the mystery out of what is about to happen and helps set the candidate at ease.

Now it is your turn. Write down some topics and ideas that you would incorporate into your opening comments.

A key part of the methodology of this kind of interview is to ask questions that seek to gain the candidate's acceptance or commitment to understanding a principle. That is why the question, "Does that make sense to you?" follows the brief introduction. This is purposely a yes or no question and it should not take much time for the candidate to make a commitment of agreement.

The act of their response preceded by the thought needed to evaluate the options on how to answer, will move the candidate in small steps to wanting to be completely truthful. Simply, the more times they say "Yes," the more effective the strategy is.

If the candidate responds in a different manner, especially by not answering the question on point, it is <u>only a warning flag</u> or an indicator that you should pay attention to and be ready to probe deeper. Though there may be good reasons why a candidate would not say "Yes" to this question, this should tell you about an avenue of inquiry that will reveal more about the candidate.

Knowing that your non-verbal communication will be heard louder than the words you say, be upbeat but serious, direct yet not arrogant and officious. Avoid crossing your arms, scowling, looking bored or leaning back like you are not interested. Be personable by leaning forward, having an open posture, smile, and be interested in them. Your attitude and demeanor will either open and widen the pathway of communication or narrow it down to a trickle of information from the candidate.

The first phase of the interview and conversation are two questions that are an evolved form of the traditional and expected, "Tell me about you" question and are intended to let the candidate "perform" with their prepared answers but with a slight twist of imposing a time limit that makes them self-edit out the unimportant information. For example, a sample question is:

"I have your application and resume. This is all that I know about you because I do not know what you told the oral interview board. So, tell me in about 120 seconds, what are the most important things that I should know about you."

This open-ended question allows the candidate to talk about themselves, which they should be prepared for, and it gives you an opportunity to judge their communication style under stress but on a topic that they should know a lot about. This is a softball question and quality candidates should be able to hit this one over the fence.

Because interviewers often "choose or snooze" in the first 90 seconds with the candidate, watch for the marginal candidate who will often struggle with this question. The "Pretender's" will be uncertain, will ramble in way that the topics do not flow to one another and their presentation will be uninteresting, if not boring. Their presentation will be disjointed and they will be unable to prioritize the most important information about themselves. The other kind of marginal candidate is the one who will talk way past the time limit, being so full of themselves, that they become lost in the moment.

The "Contender" candidate has a deep well of self-confidence to draw from. They know themselves and though humble are comfortable with their toolset, know their talents, and can articulate that they are still a work in progress on minor issues. "Pretenders" will project confidence through practice but it will be shallow and not authentic. Being open-minded, you will immediately sense who is the performing and who is genuine.

The gift of this question is to learn something about their perception of themselves; are they thoughtful, precise, and insightful; fighters or followers; leaders or pleasers; talkers or listeners?

Now it is your turn. There are other permutations of this question and the next one. Write your ideas on how you would use this theme to phrase your own question.

The next question begins to bore through the fog of "performance" behavior that most candidates bring into an interview setting. Again, it is a topic that they are familiar with:

"Tell me about the <u>real</u> you: your experience, hobbies, interest, or anything that you think is really worthy of me knowing about you."

This is the opportunity for the candidate to get to the items on their personal agenda and it has the added benefit of helping to calm them down. This is the question that the candidate should be comfortable with because it is about them; they should display their <u>best performance</u> in verbal and non-verbal communication skill and style.

In other words, if you are looking for a superior communicator, this is probably going to be the very best that they are. An old saying about job interviews is important to remember: The candidate's job performance only gets worse after the interview.

The candidate's response to this question often provides a glimpse into the side of the candidate that most employers do not know about it. You will not be intruding into the protected areas of privacy because this question is completely open-ended and the candidate can take it where they want to. The answer to this question will further personalize the remainder of the interview and conversation in a good way, two people seeking a common connection, and it sends the message that you hire complete people and not just workers; it means that you care about people and not just the work product.

However, you must be cautious with any follow-up questions or comments that you make that is based upon their answer because this can be a minefield. Stay away from the protected areas of privacy: disability, sexual orientation, religion, politics, children, marital status, race, age, and gender issues.

Sometimes, the candidate will reveal that they have been fired or they have had issues with other employers or perspective employers. They will often reveal this here because they are preoccupied with it and they want to get out at the first opportunity; thinking that if they just admit it, you will forgive them and forget about it. Of course, that is your decision but you should not compromise your standards or the organization's ethics just because you like a candidate who is sincere and apologetic. Giving second and third chances is a worthy ideal but the employment setting may not be the best place for it.

Candidates who are likable but have issues is very common and can be challenging for the executive. The more you like them, the more inclined you may be willing to overlook issues. "Pretenders" often mask their past employment problems behind sincerely delivered apologies and the lessons they learned. This is the minefield that is called, "The Likeability Index." Meaning, the more we like a candidate, the more we are blind to the signals, cues and information that they are really unsuitable for your organization.

I interviewed a candidate who had high marks from references that cited his attitude, friendliness and the ability to get along with others as his strength. His presentation skills during our conversation were stellar. However, his weakness was being nearly illiterate and struggled at constructing a paragraph. Was he sincere in his weakness? Yes. Did he offer to go to great measures to build his skill set? Yes. Was he immediately employable? No.

Be on guard for that feeling in your gut that you are overlooking issues and compromising standards and your experience by doing a "charity case" of moving forward a marginal or not-qualified candidate because you like them.

Chapter 5

LAYING THE FOUNDATION

A significant departure from the traditional interview with the organization's leadership is moving this meeting to more of a conversation about who and what the organization is really about. That is what this section and the next one is all about.

Though most candidates will have made some effort to learn about your organization, their knowledge is often extremely minimal and usually limited to a search of the Internet. From this little information, they have often created a set of assumptions and perhaps a set of dreams of what their future would look like if they were hired. This part of the conversation is intended to open their eyes to not only the strengths of your team that are unknown to nearly everyone outside the organization, but also to bluntly list the weaknesses and challenges that the employees must live with.

The value of this conversation is that it breaks the misconceptions and fantasies that the candidate may have. As a Police Chief, I have interviewed candidates who thought the agency had a SWAT team (it did not and likely would not for many years to come), who thought they would work day shift when that would not happen for years, and they could advance quickly in a matter of months instead of years. The employee who knows all the major warts of an organization at the get-go is often more willing to commit their time and energy to giving their best performance and will likely stay with the employer during the tough times.

Laying this foundation begins with using a short phrase to introduce this topic because it tells the candidate that it is time to listen to an important piece of information. For example,

"Let me talk about who we are."

At the end of the narrative that describes the organizations strengths and weaknesses, ask the question,

"Does this make sense to you?"

Now it is your turn. Write down your ideas on how to introduce this topic:

Make two columns, then <u>list the top 5 strengths</u> in one and <u>the 5 greatest challenges or weaknesses</u> in the other that every candidate should know about your organization:

This is also the opportunity to get the organization's mission and values out in front with the candidate and also summarize your organization's greatest or most recent accomplishments. For example, describe what an employee did to receive a commendation. Focus on the positives and accomplishments, not the dreams and plans for the future because the quality candidate will be swayed by concrete evidence that your team is great. Hearing this, the candidate will often be drawn to your organization and they will be more forthcoming with you in the pursuit of their desire to join it.

About the hardships and weaknesses, if there is low pay, working nights and holidays, then get it out there. You want to be realistic with the candidate and break their bubble or fantasy, if there is one. This has the intended consequence of laying the foundation early on, of what is expected of them should they be selected. Be direct, clear and cover the essential points.

Here, you do most of the talking and determine if the candidate is a listener. If the candidate is not attentive and soaking it in, if they are not listening and are only waiting for you to stop; that is a problematic behavior that will not likely go away. The marginal candidate will interrupt you to tell their story, because in their world, everything is all about them.

Your demeanor should not be apologetic or that your organization is the "victim" of budget cuts or an unsupportive community. You should be alarmed if a candidate demonstrates these themes to you because they are trying to say what they think you want to hear. "Pretenders" play the role of victims where they have no control and others are to blame for their setbacks. They will assume that you are the same way.

Be direct, neutral and matter-of-fact in your presentation of the weaknesses of the organization. You are an owner of your organization who is invested and cares deeply about it, simply behave like one.

"Contenders" are realistic and know that the world is imperfect. Though they want to join an organization that is strong, vibrant, moving forward, and founded on a clear set of principles and ethics, they want the real story that includes the blemishes. These top candidates have a depth of experience that has taught them lessons and created wisdom and you will learn this from their words and demeanor.

Again, like with the earlier questions, conclude this narrative by asking a confirmation-of-understanding question, like, **"Does this make sense to you?"** This is an important stepping-stone in their commitment to understanding and keeping them riveted to the path that you are taking them down on with this interview and conversation.

Chapter 6

THE ORGANIZATION'S PRINCIPLES AND VALUES

The next two questions are the greatest reasons why this conversation should be done with the organization's leader. This eyeball-to-eyeball dialogue between the leader and the potential new employee will do more to set the right tone, get the new employee off to the right start, and will likely do more to prevent problems than most reactive strategies. Introduce this topic with a phrase like,

"Let me tell you how you can get into trouble with me during the hiring process."

Make a brief and to the point narrative describing what the non-negotiable behaviors are, and then ask,

"Do you understand and do you have any problem with this?"

Notice the personalized phrasing of this; the intentional use of the words "you" and "me." At this point, there has been a deliberate design to

28

create trust. The candidate will likely feel a need to please you and they are bonding to you and the organization; this is a good thing and should be welcomed with genuine care.

What is needed from you and is part of your preparation is to know concisely what those non-negotiable problem areas are. For example, emphasize the need for them to be completely honest and forthcoming without even a hint of being deceptive or evasive, minimizing or exaggerating any information; that committing a crime or embarrassing the organization during the selection process will immediately disqualify them.

"Pretenders" and "Contenders" will not hesitant about agreeing to this. A warning flag is the question or remark from the candidate that redirects the conversation away from this topic or they want to narrow it to a specific time or situation. "Pretenders" use this strategy to be technically truthful or being conditional about their agreement but are not being forthcoming. A "Contender" will be clear and direct without establishing boundaries or limitations to their answer.

Now it is your turn. Make a list of those topics and behaviors that would cause you to walk away from a candidate during the selection process.

The added value with this approach is the candidate's unprepared commitment to be completely honest. You are ramping up their amount of commitment to this principle with each of their agreements. You have also plainly described the consequences of their behavior that is not honest or completely forthcoming and this will weigh heavily on the candidate's mind when you later ask a set of questions about their past behavior.

The candidate needs to fully comprehend and agree that any dishonesty, at anytime, is a predictable job-ender. If they lie now, they are out, without extensions, excuses, apologies, or exceptions. This can be very powerful stuff, not unlike the power of a taking a polygraph examination.

The next question builds upon the last one and it sets in stone the line where employees who want to stay in the organization will not cross. The question is phrased simply and directly. For example,

"Let me tell you how to get into trouble on the job."

You summarize the core values of the department in terms of performance, service and integrity, and what specific behaviors will lead to their termination. Then, like before, ask them,

"Do you understand this? Do you have any problems with this?"

Now it is your turn. Make a list of those topics and specific behaviors that would cause you to terminate any employee, without exception:

Chapter 7

DISCOVERING THE CANDIDATE'S PROBLEMATIC PAST

This is often the part of the conversation where the non-qualified candidates will provide you with the information that is later used to formally disqualify them. The notion here is to identify the ones that are marginally qualified or not qualified and you can move past them to the qualified ones.

At this stage of the conversation, most candidates have a very high desire to join your organization and they want to please you, to show their commitment and will reveal their mistakes and potentially embarrassing information. In a calm, direct, and sincere way, ask a question about the candidate's background that opens the door for them. Look at them and maintain eye contact and be sincere and interested in them during the question and their answer.

For example,

"What is in your background that you are worried about or

that I need to know about?"

For most candidates, the answer to this open-ended question will reveal what obvious issues the candidate has. Most candidates know what their problematic issues are and they have an understanding how a perspective employer may perceive this. Let the candidate fully answer the question but keep in mind that they will likely "spin" their answer that puts them in the best possible light. This is natural and is done out of self-preservation.

The "Contender" will not have any issues and that message will be delivered without hesitation and it will feel genuine. The "Contender" candidate may also talk about issues that are very minor and are not disqualifying. They will describe these because they want to be honest and completely forthcoming. The longer the life experience, the more likely there may be issues.

The "Pretender" candidate will often make small admissions and then watch and listen for your reaction and they will often adjust their delivery and the amount of admissions.

Your response and behavior should not be judgmental or emotional because the more the candidate perceives that you can handle their answer, the more they will tell you. Continue to calmly look at them, keep your hands on the table and minimize your movements. Let the candidate unwrap their package of issues and explain them while you are being open, pleasant and not judgmental.

Then, follow-up with questions that are intended to yield the specific details of where, when, who was present, and why they did it. When you have exhausted this line of questioning you need to do an assessment to determine if the conversation should end or should continue.

If they have revealed any of the mandatory disqualifiers of

selection, you can opt to plainly tell them right then, right there, that this job opportunity is not going to happen for them. How to end this conversation with dignity and respect is talked about later. Or, you can continue the conversation and gather more information while preparing yourself to deliver the news later.

In the appendix is a sample of mandatory disqualifying behaviors that one organization uses.

Now it is your turn. Begin your list of the mandatory disqualifiers for selection.

If this conversation is going to continue, be ready to ask about specific behaviors that are intended to learn about the candidate's character and judgment. One resource to draw upon in creating this area of inquiry is to use the problematic behaviors taken from a pre-employment polygraph examination to get yes or no answers. Going over these will often reveal more issues. You should be calm and detached when asking about these issues; keep it neutral and professional, not personal and do not react or be judgmental when a candidate makes an admission. Ask these questions in a slightly quicker temp and look at the candidate while they answer to receive their non-verbal messages.

A sample list of topics taken from a polygraph examination is provided in the appendix.

If the candidate answers yes to a question, again, probe deeper because their answers may disqualify them from further consideration. Most candidates are not prepared to "perform" during this line of questioning. You will likely see behaviors and hear information that are more genuine and more honest. In my experience, fully a third or more candidates will provide enough information to disqualify themselves right here.

There is a large group of candidates who are between the non-qualified and the qualified; they are the *marginally qualified*. These candidates have done things that fall into a category of behavior called "discretionary disqualifiers." These behaviors are minor violations or did not occur recently or have a mitigating circumstance. The challenge for you is to consider all these as a package and then weigh the impact and severity of these behaviors against your organization's standards and then decide if the candidate should continue with the selection process or not.

Now it is your turn. Begin your list of the organization's "discretionary disqualifiers."

Chapter 8

WHAT THE CANDIDATE REVEALS TO THE WORLD

Y ou want to know about the candidate as a "real" person, their faults, their strengths, their character and their values because these come to your organization formed by their past experiences and these will have more influence on how they perform their job than anything else. Discovering all of these characteristics in a short, "Boss' Interview" is typically not possible, but you can get a good glimpse and often more with the right questions.

At this stage of the conversation, the candidate should be on a roll of disclosing even the most embarrassing information about themselves because you have carefully laid a foundation that has created trust and confidence. Couple that with more unexpected questions and you may be surprised at what you will learn about the candidate.

You want to craft questions that are open-ended and allow the candidate freedom to answer the question in their way. Questions of a narrow scope yield narrow results. Think wider and about topics that are more vague and undefined. A good starting point for this thought process is to think of ways that people have created messages for the world to learn about them. For example,

"What emblems, decals, bumper stickers or license plate frames do you have on your car?"

This question came from an attorney who was questioning perspective jurors and it can often provide a glimpse into the candidate's values and personality. The principle here is that if a candidate is making a general statement to the world through a message posted on their car, it is open for sharing at this conversation.

I had one candidate answer this question by saying she had a bumper sticker saying, "If you going to ride my ass, then pull my hair." The follow-up question was "What is your intention of this message?" That answer provided a greater insight into the candidate's value system. The candidate was eventually disqualified because the values that led to the decision to put this bumper sticker on their car also was demonstrated in other problematic behaviors, but the first indication that there were problematic issues was that answer to this question. When you spot one weed, there will likely be others.

Many candidates have accounts with social network sites on the Internet that are public. Also, some candidates are posting blogs or contributing to forums that are available to nearly anyone to read. This information may be fair game for you to inquire about. You may be surprised by what candidates will show the world without any expectation of privacy.

Now it is your turn. List your ideas on what messages the candidate is telling the world.

Most of us have a "face" that we put on for the different roles that we live; spouse, co-worker, relative, friend, club member, etc. We do this with an expectation that people will see us in a way that meets our needs. Fully formed mature adults will acknowledge that there is often a gap between what we want people to see and how we really are; these are called misconceptions.

Asking a question about the candidate's misconceptions will often separate the mature ones from those who are less so. "Contenders" are mature candidates and the ones to hire. These candidates are realistic, know what impact they have on others and can articulate it.

The "Pretender" is marginal candidate will not have the insight into the views and perceptions of other people. They will stumble badly with this question. However, the great value of a question about misconceptions is that it allows candidates to say the truth about themselves without admitting that it is really the truth. For example,

"What are the misconceptions that people have about you?"

One candidate replied, "People think that I am moody, rigid and hard to get along with. I am not. I am focused and determined to do the job right." What do you think the interviews with the candidate's co-workers showed? Would you hire this candidate?

Chapter 9

THE FIT: DISCOVERING THE CANDIDATE'S TRUE MOTIVATION AND COMMITMENT

Pretenders and Contenders often look alike on the topics of motivation and commitment and this is what makes these interviews so difficult for the employer. This is true because of the availability of motivational books and courses and how to project confidence using keywords and non-verbal language.

"Pretenders" will have studied the <u>science</u> of succeeding at interviews but they will not demonstrate the <u>heart</u> for it However, this does not diminish the importance of tackling this during your conversation. Your organization can cause motivation and commitment to grow and blossom or it can limit and eventually kill these, but the candidate will either have these or they do not.

This section has the most questions in it because of the importance to discover the candidate's <u>motivation and commitment.</u> These are the best identifiers to determine if a candidate is a fit for your organization.

Now it is your turn. List the questions that you currently use to explore and reveal a candidate's commitment and motivation:

The easiest way to begin this topic with the candidate is to offer the expected softball question to the candidate. For example,

"Why do you want this job?"

You would think that the candidate will have a planned answer, but often when this question is asked at this part of the conversation, their answer may reveal deeper motivations. The real value will come with their answers to the follow-up questions. So, listen carefully to the candidate's initial response and then use those to probe deeper. For example, if the candidate says they want the job because they want to help people. Say, "You could help people by being a health care worker. Now, why this job?"

I interviewed a candidate who responded to this question by saying that he, "wanted to be a police officer because he liked working in a team that helped make a difference in people's lives." On the surface, that may sound like an adequate answer but by probing deeper and using an alternative job that meets the candidate's themes, the candidate will reveal more of their values behind their thought processes.

In this example, the follow-up question was, "Great answer, but why not join the fire department? They work together as a team saving lives and property. Please be more specific: why policing?" The notion here is to drill down, relentlessly and unapologetically, to the candidate's core values.

The marginal candidate will become fuzzy and generic in their ultimate response because they really do not know. Also, do not settle for the "sound bite" answer that came from the media. The "Contender" candidate will speak from heart-felt core values that will feel genuine to you. A core value is conveyed when the candidate's answer does not radically shift when it is probed and prodded from different directions.

The Substitute Question

Another effective question to discover the candidate's true motivation and commitment is to use a substitute question. The principle here is the candidate will make choices and decisions that are grounded in their motivation and commitment. With the substitute question, you take away the present job opportunity and ask the candidate to make a decision or choice and then explore their reasons behind it. The power of this question lies in two areas, the text of their answer and their non-verbal behavior during their answer. Candidates who are performing for you will often suddenly drop the act and they will behave quite differently and more genuinely. An example of the "substitute question" is,

"If you were not hired for this job, what is your Plan B?"

I love this question because the candidate's answer often shows how motivated they are and where their real passion lies. I was interviewing a candidate for a job with the police department and their response to this question was, "I always wanted to join the Navy and be at sea." This answer steered the conversation into new areas where the candidate revealed that they only applied for the job with the department due to pressure from their family.

The "Contender" candidate will answer with a heart-felt response that will leave you with the impression that they will succeed somewhere and somehow in your profession. The marginal candidate will be shallow and unfocused or their answer will be a canned sound bite that is not convincing.

When the candidate is not going to be selected for this job opportunity, this can be the theme to use as you tell them this opportunity is not going to happen for them. By transitioning the topic from one of bad news to one that, "You have the opportunity to follow your dream," can help the candidate move forward and handle the disappointment better.

Now it is your turn. Craft your own substitute question that removes this job opportunity away from consideration and the answer reveals more reasons behind the candidate's choices.

Another kind of substitute question is to create an imaginary scenario and then ask the candidate to respond with a hypothetical decision. This is a narrower question because you stay with the same profession and type of work of your organization. The goal of this question is to discover the candidate's driving ideals and powerful dreams because these are often the core drivers that create exceptional employees. An example of this question would be,

"Let's pretend for a moment that this organization does not exist and you had the ability, a magic card if you will, to work for any organization in the same profession, anywhere, and you could be in your ideal job immediately. What organization would that be and what would the job be?"

This answer will often reveal the candidate's real dreams and ambitions. If the answer is a setting that is very different from yours, there is a higher probability that the candidate will leave your organization to attain their goals. For some organizations, this may be acceptable but in others where there has been a high investment in training, this may not be an acceptable option.

You cannot predict the future but the candidate's <u>ambitions are a clue to where they are heading.</u>

Pleasantly ask for the reasons behind their choice and then drill down on them for more clarification. If their goals are in line with the opportunities that will occur with your organization, there is a higher likelihood that they will stay with you and especially during the difficult times.

If you detect that they are only "performing" to say what they think you want to hear, then they may be deceptive or evasive which is a performance trait that they will likely bring into the work place. If that is the case, consider walking away from them now while it is still easy.

Now it is your turn. Begin you <u>ideas on developing this type of alternative question</u> that best suits your situation.

The actions and decisions that the candidate has previously made are more illustrative and revealing about their motivation and commitment than anything that they promise to do in the future. When you know what organizations that they have applied to and why and then have explored what happened to that application, you are gaining a better overall picture of the candidate's values and desires. An example of this type of question is,

"What other organizations have you applied to, tested with, or are going to apply to?"

Candidates who have a long list with a wide variety of types and sizes of organizations are probably not the highest qualified candidates in the current pool. They have been passed over by other decision makers for some reason and that reason may apply to you as well. These candidates want to go anywhere and their commitment is likely thin. Do not confuse desperation with commitment. The best candidates get hired quickly.

The "Contender" or quality candidate will often have a short list or within a narrow geographic area, because they have a clear vision and therefore have a focused goal. These are the kind of employees that typically have a longer tenure with an organization.

The next approach is to have the candidate demonstrate their commitment. Words are one thing, but doing something is quite another. The notion is create an exercise where the candidate needs to read, decide and respond. An example of this is,

The Tool of the Employment Contract

When turnover is an issue in your organization or you are still uncertain about the candidate's motivation or commitment, this tool may help. Create a mock employment contract with a check box to designate a variety of the minimum years of service that they would work for your organization and tell the candidate that this is only a tool; it is not a valid contract.

The value of this tool in assessing the candidate is three-fold. First, assess the time it takes for the candidate to make a decision. A candidate who makes a quick decision or is hesitant will often have specific reasons that are worthy of exploring. Second, what the candidate's decision is. The candidate that commits to a lengthy time or a short time will have specific reasons. The candidate that does not want to sign the tool provides a reason for further inquiry. Third, the candidate's response to questions on why they chose a particular option. The notion is here is to discover the foundational reasons why the candidate makes certain choices.

An example of this tool is in the appendix.

Chapter 10

DECISION TIME: ARE THEY PRETENDERS OR CONTENDERS?

H ow will you know that this candidate should be moved out or moved forward? Though there is no formula or recipe or a scoring method to make this decision for you, there are a number of lessons-learned and words of advice from seasoned leaders who have climbed this mountain successfully. Candidates tend to fall into one of three categories:

Not Qualified

These candidates are not qualified because of the mandatory disqualifiers that they revealed during this conversation. The reasons that they made it through the other screening tests and reached you are because of their skills and likability. They will apologize for their past mistakes and will act genuinely changed because of these events. You may feel tempted to compromise the organization's standards and make an exception to hire them. Simply, <u>don't do it</u> because the costs and the risks are just too high, to you and to the organization. Saying yes is easy, saying no to a nice person who perhaps may deserve a break takes courage, but this is still the right thing to do.

I interviewed a candidate who came highly recommended by several of my employees for his ability to work with the public, work ethic and attitude. The candidate had left the profession to work in another industry. Now, he wanted to come back. During the interview, the candidate was very personable and likeable. However, he admitted to a number of behaviors that were not illegal but were against the profession's ethics. He made his case that he had learned from the mistakes, was now a convert, and swore he would never do it again. I entertained the temptation to continue the hiring process for about 90 seconds. But, I realized that if he failed, thousands of tax dollars would have been wasted and the process of hiring would start all over again and it was all preventable. Simply, he was not worth the risk.

Marginally Qualified

This category also has the most candidates, can be the trickiest to identify and takes the most courage to act on. These are the candidates who have a host of small things that tickles the hairs on the back of your neck. The most common traits are poor communicators, immaturity, questionable decisions, or personality issues that scream, "Not a Fit."

These candidates will often study the "science" of interviewing and with practice, can be good "Pretenders." They will start out strong but with time and some imposed stress, will waver, weaken and even stumble. These candidates lack depth of experience, maturity and wisdom and can be rigid.

Do not mistake IQ for maturity. A very intelligent candidate can grasp a lot of concepts and talk well but their other communication, non-verbal and the ability to self-asses, can be very limited. You will know that a candidate falls into this category when you find yourself accepting their excuses for their issues. They are always the victims of circumstances.

Do not confuse a military bearing with military discipline. The military is a great training ground and can season candidates into "Contenders." However, poor equipped candidates can come out of the military and effectively demonstrate the military bearing that masks their core faults. Exploring issues and the reasons behind their decisions will often break through this exterior.

Guard against the minefield of "likability." These marginal candidates cloak their shortcomings with a warm and engaging personality. Put the feeling that you like them aside and bore down on the data in their application: length of service, accomplishments, rewards & setbacks, gaps of employment, and reason for leaving. The truth may reveal itself with more probing.

You may find yourself "settling for" these or saying that they are "good enough" for the job. These candidates are not a good fit and you will know their shortcomings. Remember, we hire our own problems. Do you want to deal with these for a long time? Remember, the interview was the best they will ever be and if they were questionable then, the performance may be worse later.

The best words of advice are, if you do not feel excited about having this person join the organization, do not hire them.

Qualified Candidates

These are actually few and far between. Therefore, when you find one, act fast to land them. These candidates are mature, focused, genuine, committed, excited and enthusiastic, knowledgeable and well prepared. The hiring decision is actually easy when the not qualified and marginally qualified are removed from consideration.

The problem that you want is choosing between several qualified candidates for one job. In that case, it is choosing the candidate that is the right fit for the organization; who can blend in, yet complement the team with new strengths, talents and enthusiasm. Do not settle for just hiring qualified candidates; hire the ones that really "fit" your organization.

Now it is your turn. Assuming that the candidate meets all the minimum qualifications for the job, list the factors or traits that you would use in determining if the candidate is the right fit for your organization.

Chapter 11

CLOSING THE CONVERSATION & INTERVIEW

How this <u>conversation and interview ends</u> is often more important than how it started. If the candidate is not going to be moved forward in the selection process, tell them right then and there, and why. This message can be difficult to deliver and most employers will often hide their decision behind a vague letter that will require phone calls from the candidate for them to better understand the message and the reasons behind it. Unlike wine, bad news does not get better with age.

When this message is delivered plainly, directly and with compassion, the candidate is better served and it will save time by other staff members who may later field the candidate's questions. The candidate will be disappointed but this is often quickly replaced by the feeling of relief that is caused by knowing immediately what the decision is and the reasons behind it. You can compliment the candidate on their effort and offer guidance on how to succeed in the future. For example, say,

"This opportunity is not going to happen for you at this time."

After a short pause, say,

"Here is why."

Consider using the candidate's theme of what they would do if they were not hired as a source of encouragement to move forward.

Now it is your turn. *Phrase your message* *on how to tell a candidate that they are* *not going to be selected.*

If a candidate is not going to be selected, you can offer them an option to "save face" by voluntarily withdrawing from the process. Most candidates will prefer this option rather than have the record show that they were disqualified. This option also allows the employer to save time and effort in going through a formal disqualification process. A prepared leader will have a letter of voluntary withdrawal on-hand for the candidate to sign and date.

There is a sample of this letter in the appendix.

If the candidate is going to be moved forward in the selection process, provide the schedule of what will happen next and when. The prepared leader will often have the forms, letters, and information packets ready to give the candidate who is under active consideration. This sends the message that the organization is prepared and the leader is decisive.

Hiring into an organization can be a slow process that challenges the patience of candidates. Showing that the organization can be agile and timely is a reflection of the organization's professionalism. Quality candidates may have other job offers in the mix and if you really want this person, be prepared to act quickly and decisively. Today's candidates are looking for employers who can be <u>committed to them</u>.

End this conversation by showing the organization's ability to be a lasting relationship with the potential new employee. Do not let the conversation simply fade out like a racer who loses all their steam as they cross the finish line. Also, if you end the interview with, "We will get back with you," it sends a vague message that the organization may be ambivalent toward the candidate. The surest way for the candidate to be uninterested in you is to act uninterested in them.

When you end this interview and conversation with a viable and quality candidate by conveying a strong sense of confidence, support and optimism, this will help create loyalty in a new employee that may endure their whole career. The impression that you create and leave with them is the one that will be remembered, may be immortalized as they talk about it and may be the most lasting memory of how you treated them.

This is important stuff, the kind of things that great employees and great organizations are made of.

Now it is your turn, list your ideas on what you need to do to make <u>ending of this conversation</u> be the best one possible.

PART III

THE COMMAND OR LEADERSHIP INTERVIEW AS THE FINAL STEP OF SELECTION

Like many things in management, begin planning this meeting with the end in mind. Is this interview a formality because the decision has already been made? Or, are there questions that need to be resolved and decision will be made after this meeting? The answers to these questions will direct the preparation and point the way to who should be attending. Let's look at the options.

Chapter 12

THE FORMALITY INTERVIEW

You have received the thick file from the team that has evaluated the candidate. Take the time to study the components to get a feel for the candidate. Look carefully at the background investigation work to make certain that it meets or exceeds your expectations because the best predictor of a candidate's future performance is past performance in a comparable situation. Do not be shy about kicking this back for more work. If only the listed references were talked to, that is a red flag of not having the whole story.

Also, consider the theme that the further the candidate has traveled for this opportunity, the higher the likelihood that there are problematic issues to be discovered. Also, listen to the selection team to determine if they are "excited" about the candidate, because if they are <u>not,</u> this may mean there is a collection of small issues that have not been fully researched.

Use this thick pile of information to study-up on the candidate so you will act prepared for the meeting. Create a list of questions from topics gleaned from this file.

If this is truly a formality meeting with a qualified candidate and the selection team is excited about them, a powerful strategy is to invite the candidate's spouse to the meeting. Very few employers do this because they do not think of it. This sends the message that you hire more than just the candidate's skill set, you want the whole package to contribute to the organization. Spouses love it and the candidate will not only be impressed, but will likely become more invested and enthusiastic.

All the meetings I did with the candidates and spouses were very positive and every time, the spouse made a special effort to say how valuable the experience was. Spouses who understand the profession will appreciate the hard work and will be more supportive for the sacrifices necessary.

Consider having a set of bullet points for this meeting.

In the Appendix is a sample that was used by an executive of a police agency but the themes and the ideas are inspirational and transferable to other settings.

Set aside about 90 minutes for this meeting. Do the meeting in your office as it sets the tone that the candidate is entering the organization. Therefore, the office should reflect the standards and values that you want to impart: clean, neat, and organized. Your appearance should be carefully considered because you want to <u>be the attitude</u> you want to see in others.

If you want clean and professional appearance from your employees, you must model it.

Set the tone of the meeting by going to the candidate in the reception area and bring them back. Welcoming the candidate should be intentional and not delegated. Give them a warm and genuine smile, handshake, and greeting.

Give all of your attention to the candidate, treating them like they are the most important person in your life at the moment. Close the office door, turn off the phone and disable the email alert.

Consider starting the meeting with a compliment and a statement of gratitude for applying to your organization. After following the talking points, close the meeting with a brief tour of the facility and this will inspire questions from the candidate and their spouse.

Now it is your turn. What are the topics and messages that you want to include in your conversation with the employee and their spouse?

Chapter 13

THE SELECTION INTERVIEW

If you have not read the prior to two sections in this book, please do so to grasp the dynamics and help you prepare yourself and get inspired about what questions to ask. What is the purpose of this interview? Is it to determine if the candidate is qualified or when there are candidates of equal qualifications, which is the best fit for the organization? Knowing this direction, will determine how to do this interview.

You have the packet of information from the application process, and hopefully a report on the candidate's background that may include polygraph and psychological or suitability for employment reports.

The goal of this interview is typically to gauge their character, maturity, motivation, commitment, communication skills, and judgment. Create questions that draw out the candidate and these typically fall into these categories:

Insight Questions

These questions are constructed to help reveal the candidates' perception of themselves. The premise is that fully formed, mature and wise candidates make better employees. Examples:

1. *If you are not selected now, what is your Plan B for your career development?*

2. *If we talked to the co-workers who liked you the least, what would they say is your shortcomings?*

3. *The best candidates have a full compliment of experience, knowledge, skills and abilities. If you are selected, which of these is the one that you will rely upon the most and which is the one that you will need to build.*

4. *During the first two years as a new [rank or position], what do you envision will be your greatest challenges?*

Specific-Issue Questions

These are typically selected to target current issues, areas that the current employees are lacking in, and reinforcement of the agency's values or vision. These are constructed for very specific issues and topics. An example is:

This is the list of the core values of the department. Please choose one of them that is the most important to you and explain why.

Experiential Questions

These are intended to draw answers from their experience and are the best category to draw the most questions from. If you want more powerful and thoughtful answers, give the candidates the questions while they are waiting for the meeting or at least 15 minutes. Otherwise, you will get the seat-of-the-pants answers that may be shallower only because the candidate is nervous. The candidate should be able to provide a logical and concise answer with their best illustration of their knowledge, skills and abilities. The interviewers can ask the appropriate follow-up questions for clarification. Examples are:

1.   Tell us about a time where you disagreed with a supervisor's instruction or decision. What was the outcome and what did you learn from this experience?

2.   Tell us about a time where you heard employees making untrue and negative comments about [a supervisor or a co-worker]. What was the outcome and what did you learn from this experience?

3.   Explain how you have prepared yourself to assume a role of leadership within the agency. Provide examples that describe your tangible or observable efforts during the past three years and are prior to the formal announcement of this promotion process.

4.   Tell us about a difficult decision you made at work in the last year. What was the outcome and what did you learn from this experience?

Closing the interview should be more than "Thank you." This is the time to provide the capstone message, what you want the candidate to remember the most, and what impression you want them to carry out of the building with. Finish strongly, not with a fizzle, but avoid being abrupt.

Give the candidate the opportunity to make any closing remarks and to air any questions or feelings that they may have. Keep alert as how the candidate behaves and what they say, or do not say, reveals their character and their potential abilities to do the job.

This conversation does not typically end in the office. Walk the candidate out and continue to listen and offer them the opportunity to share information. Some of the best information and the candidate's real performance often happen out of the office and in the hallway.

Then, record your gut-feelings about the candidate. What did you like, what are your doubts? If you do not act on these while the information is fresh, within a few hours, 80% of the information will have faded away.

Do not make these hiring decisions alone. Have a person or two that you trust, will listen to all the positives and the doubts, who can offer clarifying questions and help you sort through the fuzziness of what information is important and which is not.

APPENDIX
Sample Interview Script

Candidate: _____ Date/Time: _____

What is the **most important thing** that I should know about you?
Tell me about you: Family, Work history, Hobbies/Interests
Tell them about the agency: Our strengths and weaknesses, what are challenges are, what we are working on, why employees want to work here
Tell them: How to get into trouble during the hiring process: Lie at anytime, do anything that creates the impression of deception or evasion, fail to keep appointments, drug use, do any crime
How to get into trouble on the job: Lie at anytime; Racism, brutality, or corruption; sex on the job; break the law; become an embarrassment to the department; fail to uphold the duty, honor and tradition of the badge
What is in your background that you are worried about or that I may be concerned about? **What else?** (Questionnaire)
What the emblems, decals, stickers and license plate frame do you have on your car?
What are the misconceptions that people have about you?
Why do you want to be (this position)?
If you were not hired as a (job), **what would you be doing?**
If not _____, and you could pick any organization, anywhere, which would that be?
Where else have you applied, tested or will be applying?
Employment Contract: check the box
What is in store for you: Go over process packet or "This is not going to happen for you today."

APPENDIX
Sample Candidate Background Questions

Have you:

Driving

How many accidents have you had

How many citations

How many times have you been stopped by the police, for what, when

When was the last time you drove while impaired

Road rage

Fastest you ever driven

Crime

Ever accused of a crime by anyone

Serious crimes that you did, though never questioned or caught

Minor crimes that you did, though never questioned or caught

Employment

Resigned in lieu of termination

Ever been fired

Purposefully did not give your full effort on an assigned task

Faked attendance records

Worked while under the influence of drugs or alcohol

Exaggerated the truth for your own self interests

Ever lied to an employer for any reason

Ever been accused of being deceptive or evasive by a supervisor

Called in sick when not sick

Taken things from an employer

Not returned any company equipment, no matter how minor

What informal coaching & counseling have you received

Ever been formally reprimanded

Domestic Violence

Ever been arrested or accused of DV

Ever been served with temporary order of protection, no contact order or anti-harassment order

Ever slapped or pushed; ever been slapped or pushed

Drugs

Last time you used any illegal drugs

Ever been told you have a drug problem

Ever used a someone else's prescription drugs

Ever injected a drug

Ever traded, concealed, transported drugs

Ever passively assisted someone else use drugs

Drinking Alcohol

How many drinks do you consume in an average week

Ever been told that you have a drinking problem

Behavior

Accused of cheating

Lost a civil suit in court

Gambling: casino or Internet

Served with a restraining or anti-harassment order

Contacted by the police for any reason

Sex with a person under 16

Peeping

Purchased sex

Last time viewed pornography on the Internet

Overcame a person's objections to have sex

Had sex while working

Used deception or lies to have sex

During this application process: lied, minimized, or exaggerated

<u>Financial</u>

Had property re-possessed

Referred to a collection agency

Had wages garnished

Filed for bankruptcy

APPENDIX

Sample Employment Contract

EMPLOYMENT CONTRACT TOOL
(This is not a valid contract and is only presented here as a tool)

WITH THE

Insert Agency's Name Here

To Whom It May Concern:

I agree and promise that if I am hired by the _____, I will faithfully perform the duties of (position here) for the _____ (this department) to the best of my ability for:

2 Years

3 Years

4 Years

5 Years

6 Years

7 Years

During this contract time, I will not seek, apply or test with any other department for the position of (Job) within (this state).

This contract is a binding agreement on my part and I enter into this deliberately, freely, willfully, and without reservation. I understand that if I breach this contract that I may have to re-pay the (jurisdiction) the costs associated with my training which will be determined by the City and may exceed several thousand dollars.

Signed

APPENDIX

Sample Letter of Voluntary Withdrawal From The Selection Process

Date:

(Hiring Authority)

(Address)

(City, State, Zip)

To Whom It May Concern:

I wish to voluntarily remove my name from the current eligibility list for (this position).

Sincerely,

APPENDIX

Sample Memorandum of Disqualifying Behaviors

To: Candidates for Employment

Subject: *BACKGROUND ISSUES THAT DISQUALIFY CANDIDATES*

We use the following guidelines for the rejection of candidates that are applying for employment with the organization. However, there may be exceptions on a case-by-case basis. Candidates who <u>fail to completely disclose</u> any of the following at the beginning of the selection process are automatically rejected. Your participation in the selection process begins with your voluntarily participation and this process is very invasive and thorough. Therefore, you should carefully consider this information and weigh this against your personal background. You may voluntarily withdrawal from the hiring process at any time.

The standard is, **"Any behavior that casts a clear doubt or suspicion on the candidate's character, integrity or competency."** Examples that may illustrate this are:

  a. <u>During the selection process:</u> failure to comply with any appointments or deadlines during the hiring process without a reasonable justification, providing false or willfully incomplete information, being evasive or deceptive at any stage in the employment process, or minimizing or exaggerating information, or failure to provide proof of attaining the minimum job requirements.

  b. <u>Crimes.</u>
   1. Committing a felony crime or any crime of moral turpitude, regardless if convicted, charged or officially reported to a police agency with in the past 10 years,
   2. Unless otherwise described below, any misdemeanor crime regardless if convicted, charged or reported to a police agency within the past 3 years, or
   3. Patterns of misdemeanor criminal behavior as an adult or within the past 5 years.

c. Behavior that casts reasonable doubt regarding issues of integrity, for example, as falsifying work attendance records, filing false claims, making an intentionally false statement on an official document or employment-related document, cheating or dishonesty.

d. Committing domestic violence that would be considered a misdemeanor regardless if reported to a police within the previous 5 years.

e. Addictive Behavior that could reflect poorly on the organization or illustrate bad judgment on the part of the candidate, for example, drugs, alcohol, sex, pornography, gambling.

f. Legal inability to own or possess a firearm (if this is a job requirement).

g. Illegal Drugs. The use, possession, or sale of controlled substances under these circumstances:
   1. Illegal drug use that is isolated or low frequency within the past 3 years,
   2. Illegal drug use that is high frequency within the past 10 years,
   3. Participating in the manufacture, selling, offering to sell, trading for, distribution, or transportation for sale any illegal narcotics or prescription drugs regardless of time frame,
   4. Use of illegal drugs while employed in any position of public trust regardless of time frame,
   5. Use of a prescription drug through fraud or deception, regardless of time frame, or
   6. Working under the influence of drugs, alcohol or non-prescription drugs within the past 5 years.

h. Driving. Pattern of driving behavior that casts doubt upon the candidate's judgment. Examples are:
   1. Within the past 5 years: criminal offenses regardless of being arrested or cited, road rage, 5 or more traffic citations, history of repeated cancelled auto insurance, license was suspended or revoked or five or more traffic crashes, or
   2. Conviction of Driving Under the Influence of Intoxicants within 5 years and this includes receiving a diversion or a plea

to lesser charge or two or more convictions regardless of time frame

i. Military Service: dishonorable discharge, did not complete enlistment, or not eligible for re-enlistment.

j. Medical: concerns or problems that might endanger the candidate, fellow employees or citizens, or the inability to perform the essential job functions as described in the job description.

k. Work history that reflects dishonesty, disloyalty, incompetence, instability, dereliction of duty, or inability to get along with supervisors or co-workers, pattern of unexcused absences, involuntarily termination for cause, resignation in lieu of termination, or discipline that is 2 or more formal reprimands.

l. Failure to provide proof of United States citizenship.

m. Financial affairs that show a history of poor judgment, irresponsibility or refusal to confront problems such as referral to collection agency, property re-possessed or wages garnished.

n. Misrepresentation or ignoring laws such as not paying taxes or using a false address for school tuition purposes.

o. References. People who know the candidate doubt the candidate's honesty, self-discipline, judgment or character.

p. Psychological Fitness.
   1. Candidates who are rated by a licensed Psychologist as "low average" or lower, or are marginally suited for law enforcement or who have significant moderate psychological concerns that could present a clear and specific risk to themselves, the public or to other employees within the past year.
   2. History of anger or emotional issues that show instability, impulsiveness or could present risks to themselves, the public or to other employees.

For Experienced Police Officers, in addition to the above:

q. Any behavior that would be considered a minor violation of the policies of the <u>your agency Police Department</u> within the past 3 years

r. Any behavior that would be considered a moderate or severe violation of the policies of the <u>your agency Police Department</u>, regardless of time frame

Failure to meet the minimum performance standards of the agency of employment or of the <u>your agency Police Department</u> within the previous 3 years.

APPENDIX

Sample Talking Points for Candidates and Spouse Meeting

First, I want to welcome you to our organization and our team. We may be hiring your spouse, but we are accepting your entire family into our profession.

1. We provide the finest equipment and training available

2. We have an outstanding group of employees

3. We believe in the safety of our employees before the safety of anybody else.

4. We have an incredible group of spouses and families that have several organized events per year.

About the training:

1. Three Field Training Officers will be guiding you through the process. But the burden to succeed is yours.

2. The academy will be very hard on the family. You must be prepared for that.

3. The stress and the demands will require sacrifices that some are unwilling to pay.

4. No Officer has failed the academy under my watch.

About being a Police Officer:

1. You are entering a world where the expectations are different.

2. After you have completed the apprenticeship portion of your training, the performance expectations are very high: When others can get angry-you must be calm; when others can avoid conflict-you must confront it; when others can run from danger-you must approach it.

3. You must constantly keep yourself mentally, emotionally and physically prepared.

4. When disaster hits, you do not have the option of staying home. Your family will have to contend with emergencies without you and they must be prepared for it.

5. You are not required to carry a weapon off-duty, but many employees have one accessible to them. That means having a firearm around your family and the necessity of taking certain precautions. You are not required to keep your duty weapon at home but if you do, we will provide a lock box for you.

6. Everything we do is confidential in the details. Share with your family the events and your feelings but not the names nor addresses nor any detail that can be traced to a specific person.

7. Overtime is not a way of life, but it is sometimes essential and may be done without notice.

8. Your personal appearance becomes official business

About your personal life:

1. You must be ready to share your reactions and feelings with your spouse who is your main team member.

2. People will hold you to a different standard. Both on-duty and off-duty. Both good and bad.

3. You will be stereotyped and pre-judged. Some will be attracted to you, others will be repelled.

4. Your spouse will often be treated as a source of information about policing.

5. Your life may become a fishbowl.

6. Your children may be treated differently in school.

7. A 12-hour shift may become a 15-hour one and the personal plans will have to adjust.

8. Most everyone works the 4th of July, so you can kiss your family plans good-bye.

9. Half of the officers work the normal holidays.

10. You cannot do anything that will bring dishonor to the tradition of the profession or to this profession.

11. If you embarrass yourself professionally, you embarrass this department and those who have served honorably before you-and I will not have it.

12. Being seriously injured or killed is a remote possibility and your family must have a plan for that. Your may choose to participate in a "Confidential Information" program where your personal information and wishes are described and locked in my office.

13. The total package of this occupation is a great strain on relationships and can shorten your life unless you protect yourself mentally, emotionally and physically; share the burden and work together.

Finally:

1. This business provides a front row seat to the greatest show on earth. You will see things, meet people, and encounter events that no one else will do.

2. You are not in this adventure alone.

3. These are the immediate resources available to you: me and the whole supervisory team, our department chaplains, the Employee Assistance Program; the spouse's group

If you are concerned about anything, call me directly.

ABOUT THE AUTHOR

John Gray served in the law enforcement profession for 32 years, including 12 years as a Police Chief in Washington State in two cities. He has worked for city, county and federal agencies in both urban and rural settings. He has extensive experience, training and education in the management of an agency.

He has a Masters in Education from Western Washington University and Bachelor of Arts from San Diego State University. He is an active member of the International Association of Police Chiefs. He is a life member of the Washington Association of Sheriff's and Police Chiefs.

John Gray taught management topics for the Northwestern University's School of Police Staff and Command and was a part-time community college instructor for 10 years teaching criminal justice courses. He is on the faulty of Western Illinois University's Executive Institute that provides leadership and command training to public safety agencies.

He continues to teach or guest lectures for criminal justice training agencies and organizations on the topics of budgeting, leadership, and supervision.

He has published articles on management topics in FBI Bulletin, Police Chief Magazine, Law & Order Magazine, Police Fleet Manager, and Public Manager Magazine.

A current list of presentations and publications are available on his website at: www.johnlgray.net
Email: jlgraycompany@clearwire.net

Fun fact: An avid boater, he and his wife Laurie have published articles on their cruising experiences. See their boating websites, www.andiamo-ranger29.com and www.laurieann-ranger25.com

www.ingramcontent.com/pod-product-compliance
Lightning Source LLC
Chambersburg PA
CBHW070231210526
45168CB00020B/2024